Marco Polo

Betty Lou Kratoville

ORDER DIRECTLY FROM
ANN ARBOR PUBLISHERS LTD.
P.O. BOX 1, BELFORD
NORTHUMBERLAND NE70 7JX
TEL. 01668 214460 FAX 01668 214484
www.annarbor.co.uk

International Standard Book Number: 1-57128-167-3

9 8 7 6 5 4 3 2
0 9 8 7 6 5 4 3 2

Contents

CHAPTER 1

Growing Up in Venice

Marco Polo was born at the right time in the right place to the right family. His birthplace was Venice on the east coast of Italy. The year was 1254. What a grand city Venice was in those days – busy, colorful, exciting – a great spot for a boy to grow up.

Venice was perched on the edge of the Adriatic Sea. Indeed, one might say she "floated" on the sea. Most of her streets were canals. On them fleets of bright gondolas glided.

Venice was then called "queen of the sea." Her docks were always jammed. Ships came from all over the known world. Ships laden with spices, ivory, and slaves. There was a good reason why Venice was a center for trade. Location! It could easily be reached by land and by sea, by ship and by packhorse or camel.

Venice was at peace most of the time. Now and then she had a scrap with Genoa, a city on the west coast of Italy. These clashes didn't last long. They didn't upset the rich flow of life in Venice. Kings and princes in other cities and countries often fought with one another. Not Venice! She just kept tending to business and getting richer and richer.

Crusaders stopped there on their way to the Holy Land. They needed food, arms, and supplies. The merchants in Venice were happy to provide them – for a price!

The young Marco grew up in all of this splendor. He watched noblemen build palaces along the Grand Canal. He heard music pouring from cool, dim churches. He went in shops and markets that bulged with goods to fit everyone's purse. He enjoyed parades with clowns and minstrels. The rich ladies were a sight to behold! They were clad in silks and jewels. On their feet they wore clogs built like stilts. Some were three feet high! Why these odd shoes? Because the unpaved streets were so muddy! In time the dangerous clogs were banned.

Marco's father, Nicolo, and his uncle, Maffeo, were merchants. They often were away on long trips. Marco was born shortly before his father left on a trip to Constantinople (now Istanbul). While Nicolo was away, his wife died. Marco went to live with an aunt. At that time there were few schools in Venice. Marco was left free to wander around the lively city. He came to know Venice well and to love it.

For years he did not know where his father and uncle were. Were they still alive? He could not be sure. But then one day when he was 15 years old, the door opened, and there they stood! Such an unexpected, welcome surprise – and even more surprising – they had been all the way to China! Few people had been that far before. The two Polos had stayed at the court of the great Kublai Khan!

Another surprise – they were going back. Kublai Khan had asked them to do him a favor. As the ruler of all China, he had great power and wealth. He also had a curious mind. He wanted to know all about people in other lands. He had sent the Polo brothers with a letter to the Pope. In it he asked that 100 churchmen be sent to China. These men had to possess vast knowledge and great wisdom. The Pope could spare only two men. In fact, not too many churchmen were eager to travel all the way to China.

It took two years to get ready for the journey. During that time, Nicolo married again. Marco had a home of his own for the first time in years.

At last the two Polos started out. With them were two friars sent by the Pope. Best of all, in the group was a joyful Marco, who was then 17 years old. He had been thrilled when his father and uncle invited him to go along. Little did he guess that he would be gone for 24 years!

They did not get off to a good start. They bumped right into a war. The two friars looked at one another. Was this the way the whole trip would be? They grabbed their baggage and rushed back to Venice. The three Polos decided to keep going.

The Polos set out on their trip.

CHAPTER 2

On the Road

The first important stop was Jerusalem. The Chinese ruler, Kublai Khan, had asked the Polo brothers to bring him oil from the lamp that hung above the tomb of Christ. They had failed to bring him 100 churchmen. They wanted badly to fill his second request. And it proved to be quite easy to get the oil.

With the Khan's gift in hand, they headed for a city on the Persian Gulf. They had hoped to find a ship there. A week went by. They looked at all kinds of ships in the harbor. None would do. "These would shatter in the first storm," said Nicolo. So the Polos made up their minds to go by land. They learned that the safest way to travel was by caravan. They found one that was just about to leave.

Weeks went by as they plodded along mile after mile. Marco was amazed by the cities they passed. Some were high in the mountains. It was too cold there even for birds. Some were perched on the edge of a desert. Sand storms were a way of life for them. Most cities were hidden behind high walls. None were the least bit like the elegant Venice that Marco remembered.

One city, they were told, was the home of the

three wise men who had followed the star to Bethlehem. The three men were buried there in a great tomb. Many visitors came to see it.

The Polo caravan also passed near Mount Arafat. The people who lived nearby said that this was where Noah's Ark had come to rest after the flood. It was a high mountain – 17,000 feet. No one had ever climbed it. Finally, many centuries later, someone reached the top. No Ark! But chunks of fossilized wood were found. How did they get there?

One new sight followed another. Marco saw a geyser that gushed oil. Dozens of camels were needed to carry it away. It was used to light lamps and as an ointment to treat skin rashes. Marco wondered, did no one in Europe know about this precious resource?

The caravan covered about 10 miles a day. One day it came to a region known for its tribes of thieves. Sure enough! The Polo caravan was attacked as a dust storm swirled around them. The attack came as such a surprise, the men in the caravan could not fight back. Animals and goods were scattered near and far. Some members of the caravan were killed. Others were taken prisoner to be sold into slavery. Somehow the Polos got away and fled to a nearby small village. There they waited for another caravan.

At last they came to the great Gobi Desert. It was by far the most dangerous part of their trip.

They rested for a week before starting out. They loaded their camels with food and water. They tied bells around the animals' necks so they would not get lost. There were 20 oases in the Gobi. Each one had only a small supply of water, and it was often bitter. No birds, no animals. Just bleached bones of travelers. A man had to be careful not to fall behind the caravan. If he lost sight of it, he might wander for days. Death would surely follow.

They crossed the Gobi at its most narrow point. Even then it took them 30 days. During this crossing they had been in the land of the Mongols. Not so long ago the Mongols had been greatly feared. And for good reason. They had once been a warlike people who came very close to overrunning all of Europe. It is thought that only the death of their leader caused them to change their minds and turn back. Had this savage leader not died, the history of Europe might have been very different.

The Mongols that Marco Polo saw were nomads. Mostly they wandered from place to place looking for grass for their animals. They lived in huge tents made of felt. When they moved, the tents were carried on carts as wide as 25 feet between the wheels. Sometimes it took 22 oxen to pull these heavy carts.

The Mongols ate mostly meat. Even cats, dogs, and rats if their supply of large animals was low. They ate with their hands. Then they wiped their greasy fingers on their shoes or boots. This kept the leather soft and easy to wear for days at a time. They packed strips of dried meat and cakes of dried milk in their saddlebags. On freezing days a Mongol soldier would open a vein in his pony's leg. Then he would drink its warm blood. No wonder people in Europe had been terrified of the thought of the savage Mongols!

The best known Mongol soldier had been Genghis Khan. At one time Genghis Khan had gathered an army of 129,000 men and 390,000 horses. This army surged across Asia. It burned and plundered as it went. It is thought that millions of people were killed while Genghis was in power.

At the time the Polos went to China another Mongol leader, Kublai Khan, ruled the land. But he was a man of peace. He had so much power he feared no one, least of all a trio of men from Venice.

CHAPTER 3

China!

The overland trip had been long and slow. Bad weather often held up the caravan. They stopped in some cities for months when the trading was good. There came a day when Marco grew very ill. The Polos stayed in that town for a year while he got better.

The three men had been on the road for more than three years. They needed only about 40 more days to reach Peking in far east China. Imagine their surprise when they were met by a large

Marco Polo welcomed at the Court of Kublai Khan.

escort sent by the great Kublai Khan.

The escort led them to the Khan's summer palace north of Peking. The sound of trumpets filled the air. Everyone was dressed in royal robes. A welcome fit for a king!

Kublai Khan was pleased to see Nicolo and Maffeo again. He pointed to Marco. "Who is this young man?" he asked.

Nicolo bowed. "This is my son who will serve you well," he said.

A great banquet was held in honor of the return of the Polos. Marco was soon given a high place in the Khan's court. He had never seen such splendor nor such strange customs. His eyes grew wide when he watched the Khan drink from a gold cup. Everyone knelt, and a band played until the Khan put his cup down.

Marco had learned to speak Mongol on the long journey. He quickly picked up the Chinese court's customs and manners. He and Kublai became good friends. The Khan took him hunting. Ten thousand men went with them to make sure the hunt was a success. Marco looked around him. Would people at home ever believe all this?

It was clear Kublai trusted the young man. He sent him on important errands. He let him travel freely. Marco put his reports in story form. The Khan loved to read them.

Marco traveled in comfort on his trips. The

Khan saw to that. The young man was carried in a handsome sedan chair. He had servants to wait on him. He had soldiers to keep him safe on the road. Everywhere he went, there were astonishing things to see and learn about.

What was this? Money made from paper? Metal coins were still used in Venice and the rest of Europe. Coins were heavy and bulky to carry. Paper money was light. Marco overlooked one important point. Chinese paper money was *printed*. Printing did not appear in Europe for two more centuries. But somehow Marco took no notice of the printing on the Chinese money.

Another wonder – black stones that burned! Marco saw men digging these stones out of the ground. A stack of them would burn through the night. Much better than wood, he thought. The Chinese used these black stones to cook and heat water. They bathed often – sometimes every day. In Europe people seldom took a bath. Instead they used a lot of perfume.

One other marvel – the Chinese had fireworks, all kinds. Marco never grew tired of watching them on holiday nights.

Kublai chose Marco to make a tour of some of his states. It took him four months to reach Yunnan in the southwest and then onto Burma farther south. Each day brought dazzling new sights – craggy mountains, fertile valleys, winding rivers, strange customs. Marco found one tribe in Burma that had a most odd tradition. A child was born. Then its father stayed in bed with the new baby for 40 days. During this time the mother took care of both of them. It was felt this would build a bond between father and child.

One would not have wished to be a stranger in Burma. At least not a stranger with a kind heart and a good character. The Burmese thought that a person's bright spirit and good qualities stayed with the family in whose home he was slain.

Marco's second long trip for Kublai Khan took him southeast to Mangi. Marco served as governor of this rich state for a short time. He was impressed with the Yangtze River when he crossed it. In places it looked more like a wide sea than a river. He guessed that on some days there were as many as 15,000 ships on that river.

This trip included a stop at Kinsai. Marco liked this large city because it made him think of home. It had many canals just like Venice. It was as easy to get around by water as it was by land. Most of the houses of Kinsai were built of wood. They tended to catch fire easily. The Kinsai people were expert at fighting these fires. A watchman stood on every main bridge. When he sighted a fire, he beat on a wooden drum. The watchmen on all the other bridges ran to help put out the fire.

Marco liked Kinsai for its parks, its well-paved streets, its crowded markets. He did not learn that Kinsai was a center for the arts. He never saw its libraries that held more books than any other city in China. This at a time when there were almost no books in all the rest of the world.

CHAPTER 4

India

When the Khan sent him to India, Marco was spellbound by the country and its people. He learned as much as he could about its Buddhist religion. He admired the teachings of the Buddha who had begun it. He was moved by its pilgrims. They came from near and far. They wanted only to pray on the mountain where the Buddha had lived and died 500 years ago.

In the very hot part of India, Marco saw people who wore no clothes except a loincloth.

Their king followed this custom, too. But he also wore all sorts of jewels. He had a collar of diamonds around his neck. He had gold bracelets on both arms and legs. His fingers glittered with heavy rings. Most important of all, he wore a necklace of 104 pearls and rubies. Each jewel stood for one prayer he had to say every day. Think of it – 104 prayers daily!

This king had 500 wives! Noblemen in his court went everywhere with him. When he died, he was cremated. His nobles leaped into the fire. They felt that in this way they could follow him into the next life.

Marco did not always agree with India's strange ways. He thought some of them were downright cruel. When a husband died, his wife was supposed to throw herself on his funeral fire. Many women did so. (It was said that some of them had to be drugged first.) Those who did not join their husbands in death were scorned by family and friends for the rest of their lives.

In Europe people seldom washed. Marco found that in India the natives washed their bodies twice each day — once before they ate in the morning, once before their meal at night. Everyone had his own cup. A native would not drink from a cup owned by any other person, and they did not let their lips touch the cup. They held it above their heads. Then they poured the drink in a stream into their mouths.

The way Indians took care of owing money seemed odd to Marco. The creditor would draw a circle around the debtor. The debtor could not leave the circle until he paid his debt. It did not matter if the person were a king or a commoner. The rule was used for all. It worked!

Marco visited diamond fields. He was stunned by the size of the diamonds mined there. He also traveled to a place where two castes (groups) lived. The first group he met were the Brahmins. Marco felt they were the most honest people in the world. They did not lie. They did not cheat. They hated all killing. If an animal needed to be killed, they asked someone who was not a Brahmin to do it. They had deep faith in signs and omens. Shadows and sneezes and spiders all had a special meaning for them.

Then there were the Yogis. Marco took notes about their strange ways. He was sure the people back home would not believe him. Perhaps his notes would help. It is a fact that the ways of the Yogis were very strange. First of all, they wore no clothes – not a stitch! They felt everyone should go about in the state in which he or she was born. They worshiped the ox. Every Yogi wore an image of the ox on his forehead. They used dried leaves for plates. They would not kill anything, not even a worm. They ate no meat, only dried plants and roots. They drank nothing but water. Their life span was many years longer than those of people in Europe. Might their lifestyle have something to do with this?

In the Indian city of Ceylon, Marco liked to watch the pearl divers. These men and boys dived to a depth of six fathoms (about 36 feet). The oysters they brought up were opened and set in tubs of water. When they rotted, the soft parts floated to the top. The pearls stayed at the bottom of the tubs. Sharks would sometimes wander into the waters where the divers worked. Their bosses hired Brahmins to cast a spell to keep the sharks away. This custom must have worked, for it went on for hundreds of years.

Marco's notebooks grew fuller and fuller. He would have many stories to tell.

CHAPTER 5

Going Home

Nicolo and Maffeo met one day to talk. As always, they agreed with one another. They felt it was time to think of going home. They had been gone for more than 20 years. Their stay in China had been good. They had kept busy. They had lived a rich life. They had seen places and things never dreamed of. Yet they missed their families and life in Venice.

There were other things to think of. Kublai Khan was now 75 years old. He might die at any time. What would happen to the Polos then? Who would be their new ruler? Would he be as kind to the Polos as Kublai had been? They would have liked to talk this over with Marco but he was in India. They did not know when he would be back.

They went to see the Khan. They needed his consent to leave China. The Khan was not pleased. Why did they want to go? Did they want wealth? He would give it to them. Did they want honors? He would see that they got them. He asked them to wait. Nicolo and Maffeo had no choice. The Khan's word was law. They tried to be patient. Perhaps Marco could help them when he got back.

Then a stroke of luck came their way. A ruler

named Arghun was the Khan of Persia. His favorite wife, Bolgana, died. She left one wish. She wanted his next wife to come from her family in Mongolia. Arghun had loved his wife. He wanted to grant her last wish. He sent three men to Peking. Would his friend Kublai please find him a new wife from Bolgana's family in Mongolia?

Kublai chose a princess, Cocachin, to take Bolgana's place. She and the three men sent by Arghun started out for Persia. They took many servants and guards with them. War had broken out along the caravan routes. They could not get through. They had to return to Peking.

By this time Marco had come back from

India. He had taken a water route. It had been a safe and easy trip. It would be a fine way to get Princess Cocachin to Persia if Marco would agree to serve as a guide.

The plan was told to Kublai Khan. He was not pleased with it. But he knew he had to somehow get the princess to Persia. At last he agreed. At once he became the kind, generous ruler the Polos had always known. He gave them a gold tablet to ensure a safe journey. He filled their trunks with costly clothes and jewels. Best of all, he gave them 13 huge Chinese ships. He stocked them with supplies to last two years. The ships were large four-masters. They had crews of two or three hundred men.

The fleet of 13 ships left China in the spring of 1292. It took two years through storms, scurvy, heat, and other hardships to reach Persia. Six hundred people had died along the way. The news in Persia came as a shock. Arghun Khan, who had sought a new wife, was dead. What to do? Cocachin, who had come to be his wife, married his son instead.

The Polos rested in Persia for nine months. While there, they heard that Kublai Khan had died. They grieved for their friend but they were glad they had left China when they did. They could not help but wonder what the new ruler might be like.

Homeward bound again and more troubles.

At a stop on the Black Sea they were robbed of much of their money and goods. A few more stops and then at long last they saw the domes of Venice. The trip home had taken three years.

They had been gone so long their family and friends did not know them. Their clothes were shabby and worn from the long trip. Their speech was rough. Marco had been 17 when he left. Now he was 41. He had taken the longest journey in history. He had seen more of the world than any man of his time.

The Polos gave a large banquet. They served the best foods and wines. They brought out trunks full of the beautiful gifts Kublai Khan had given them. It was then that the people of Venice began to treat them with respect and to believe their stories.

It was time to settle down for Nicolo and Maffeo. But not Marco! Venice and Genoa were once more at war. Marco was put in command of a long, low ship that would take part in the sea war. What did fate still have in store for him?

CHAPTER 6

Prison!

Marco and the men of Venice fought bravely. But courage was not enough. Genoa won the battle at sea and took many prisoners. One of these was Marco. He was put in a tower. Perhaps it was better than a cell. But the days dragged on and on.

There was nothing to do. Marco was bored and restless. One day to pass the time he told a story about his China trip to his fellow prisoners. They asked for more. Marco was willing. It made the long days go by faster. Word spread. The people of Genoa started coming to the prison to hear the tales.

One of the prisoners had been there for a long time. His name was Rustichello. Before he was captured, he had been a writer. He had written about King Arthur and the Knights of the Round Table. He was one of the men who gathered around Marco.

One day Rustichello had an idea. If Marco were willing, Rustichello would write down his stories. That sounded good to Marco! He had so much to tell. It was clear he had to have help to get it all down in good order. He also needed his trunkful of notes. He wrote to his father. Nicolo sent the notes at once.

Rustichello and Marco worked well together. The book they wrote was clear and colorful. They called it *The Travels of Marco Polo*. Marco put in everything he could remember. On the other hand, he left out a lot. He said not a word about the Great Wall of China or the use of chopsticks or the custom of binding girls' feet or printed books. Perhaps through the years these things had become so common to him, he didn't think them worth mentioning.

Just as the book was finished, Venice and Genoa made a truce. All of the prisoners of war were let go. Marco went home to Venice as fast as he could get there.

Of course, he took the book manuscript with

A page from Marco Polo's book.

him. Copies of it were quickly made in Italian and Latin. Word about the book spread. In the next years it was translated into Spanish, German, and Irish. Even so, copies were few and far between. Then in the mid-15th century, Johannes Gutenberg invented the printing press. Soon *The Travels of Marco Polo* could be found all over Europe.

Some readers had doubts. They could not believe all that Marco had written about China's wealth and splendor. Many were sure he was lying. But people like Christopher Columbus read it, and they believed it from beginning to end.

During these years China changed greatly. The Mongols no longer ruled. Now the Chinese had taken control of the country. They did not like strangers. They sent foreigners home. They stopped all trade by closing ports. At the same time, the Turks were raiding the overland caravans. The doors to China were closed. That meant that the Polos had been some of the very last men to be welcomed at Peking. Marco was one of the first and the last to know enough to write about it.

Shortly after he got back to Venice, Marco married. He and his wife had three daughters. He took up trading again. He traded with Russia for furs. He traded with England for tin and wool. Marco had not lost his touch. He made a good living for his family. Even so, his life must have seemed dull after the thrills of life in Peking.

Marco Polo lived to be 70. A ripe old age in those days! As he lay dying, a priest leaned over him. "My son," he said, "do you want to take back any of the tall tales in your book?"

Marco answered in a whisper. "I did not tell half of what I saw, for I knew I would not be believed."